THE COUNTRY DIARY®

Calligraphy

Projects by Ann Bowen and Gail Glaser
Original illustrations by Edith Holden

The Country Diary of an Edwardian Lady®
© Rowena Stott (Designs) Ltd and RW.UK Ltd 2006
Licensed by ©opyrights Group

Original illustrations by Edith Holden

KUDOS

First published in Great Britain in 2006 by Kudos, an imprint of Top That! Publishing plc,
Marine House, Tide Mill Way, Woodbridge, Suffolk IP12 1AP, UK
www.kudosbooks.com

0 2 4 6 8 9 7 5 3 1

ISBN 1-84666-022-X

A catalogue record for this book is available from the British Library
Colour reproduction by Reflex Reproduction
Printed and bound in China

Acknowledgments and Credits:
Managing Director Barrie Henderson
Kudos Manager Mike Saiz
Designer David Freeland
Senior Editor Karen Rigden
Junior Editor Duncan Ballantyne-Way
Photographer Jo Broome
Project calligraphy by Ann Bowen
Project illustrations by Gail Glaser
Picture Credits: p 3; Werner Foreman Archive. p 4; Topham Picture Point. p 6; Ancient Art
and Architecture Collection. p 8; Topham Picture Point. p 12-13; Jupiter images.

Contents

Introduction

Calligraphy, the art of beautiful writing, is a captivating craft and art form that is a pleasure to do and, once perfected, can be used to create stunning and memorable gifts and projects.

In today's technological age, with all its computerised fonts, it would be easy to regard calligraphy as an outmoded art form. However, this captivating craft continues to fascinate generation after generation.

The appeal of calligraphy may lie in the sense of satisfaction gained from creating something beautiful, or from the versatility of the skills which can be applied to glass, china, wood, cloth and even on walls, as well as the conventional use of lettering on paper and card.

This is a beginner's guide, for those who know nothing about calligraphy and have never tried to produce this 'beautiful writing' (the literal meaning of the word 'calligraphy').

Many cultures have a rich history of writing techniques, but in this book we have worked with only the Western styles.

With advice on what equipment to buy, how to use it and even how to make money from your new skill, this book will be your entry into the art of calligraphy.

The Country Diary

Calligraphy has been inspired by the elegance and beauty of *The Country Diary of an Edwardian Lady*®.

Coupling the beauty of calligraphy with original artwork inspired by the stunning paintings of Edith Holden's diary, this book demonstrates just some of the creative possibilities this time-honoured craft can offer.

Edith Holden: A Brief Biography

Edith Holden, was born in 1871. In her lifetime she was an artist and art teacher. She was also well known as an illustrator of children's books. Although *The Country Diary of an Edwardian Lady* was published in 1977, it is actually a naturalist's diary for the year 1906. In the course of that year, Edith recorded the seasonal changes of the British countryside in words and delicate, delightful watercolours.

When it was rediscovered and published in the seventies, readers were captivated by its charm and evocation of a simpler world. It has now been translated into 13 different languages and sold millions of copies worldwide.

Tragically, Edith was to die in 1920, at the age of 49. Collecting flowers from a riverbank at Kew Gardens in Richmond near London, she fell into the River Thames and drowned.

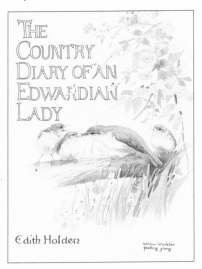

THE COUNTRY DIARY OF AN EDWARDIAN LADY

Edith Holden

Willow Warbler feeding young.

A Brief History of Calligraphy

The word calligraphy comes from the Greek 'kale graphe', which means 'beautiful writing'. There are three main styles of calligraphy today: Chinese (Oriental), Arabic and Western. These styles developed independently, but, as early manuscripts spread around the world, styles began to influence each other.

The Evolution of Calligraphy

All calligraphy evolved from ancient forms of writing such as Egyptian hieroglyphics and Chinese pictograms. In early society the ability to read and write was the domain of the priests or other religious scholars and, as such, most writing was devoted to religious texts and subjects.

The desire to produce 'beautiful writing' came from the belief that the word of God was sacred, and that the expression of God's word should be suitably beautiful.

The ultimate expression of this belief is found in the illuminated manuscripts of the medieval monks who produced masterpieces such as the Irish *Book of Kells* (see right), still preserved in Dublin.

Calligraphy, however, has never been a purely Christian practice. Islamic scholars laboured to produce copies of the Qur'an using exquisite gold inks and rich colours. Islam's proscription on depicting images of living creatures meant that calligraphy from the Arabic lands developed a unique graphic language of pattern and colour, while Western decorative styles were based around local flora and fauna. Today, modern Arabic script shows its calligraphic heritage clearly in its organic letter forms and elegant flourishes.

Chinese calligraphy is probably the oldest form of calligraphy, with some scholars dating it at over 4,000 years old. While languages such as English, Russian and Japanese are based around representing sounds (phonetic), Chinese and ancient Egyptian scripts represent meaning (ideographic). Chinese is the only surviving ideographic language and, as such, is uniquely suited to the expressiveness of calligraphy.

The Fall and Rise of Calligraphy

The invention of the printing press eventually removed the need for individually hand-lettered books, but for many years early printing could not match the fine detail of the best calligraphy, and skilled calligraphers remained in demand. However, as presses improved, calligraphy retreated more and more into the domain of amateurs and artists.

Another, less dramatic, technical change was the introduction of the round-nibbed pen, similar to the modern fountain pen. This change from the flat, square nibs that had been in use before made it difficult to achieve calligraphic letter forms in everyday writing. Therefore, the skill began to die out.

In China, calligraphy, along with poetry and painting, is still considered an essential indication of character. In imperial times, positions in the Court and government were allocated to those who could produce perfect writing as it was considered that someone unable to compose precise, legible writing was not to be trusted with such important matters as taxation and accounting!

Ancient Chinese masters of calligraphy are as revered today as they were generations ago. It is accepted that there are four great schools of calligraphy – Yan, Liu, Ou and Zhao – each with their own distinctive character.

Art Form

Calligraphy is now a popular and growing hobby but it is not just limited to this. There are traditions in Japan of new students writing large calligraphic characters on huge banners at the beginning of the school year. In China the art of calligraphy is often considered to be on an equal footing with painting. Here it is used as a means to connect Chinese schoolchildren to their cultural history. Calligraphy is still considered an art form, not just in Asia, but all over the world.

The ability to produce beautiful writing in an age when most letters are typed, and e-mail is more widespread, is becoming recognised as a valuable skill. With the whole history of calligraphy available to the practitioner as inspiration, new forms are being created. In our modern computer era it may be that calligraphy begins to enjoy a new golden age.

Using Calligraphy Today

Finding a place for calligraphy in the modern world is easier than it may seem. The projects featured later in this book demonstrate a variety of uses but here are other ideas than may inspire and encourage you.

Edward Bulwer-Lytton famously wrote that 'the pen is mightier than the sword'. Few could argue with his sentiments, and the captivating power of calligraphy certainly supports the cause. Even today a beautifully handwritten piece of prose has the power to move most people whether they are looking at an ancient, illuminated script or a modern, decorated poem.

For many, calligraphy is reserved for special occasions in the making of wedding invitations or thank you notes, and indeed crafting such work, once your skills have been perfected, can be a good way to earn additional money. It is easy to put your new skills to more use, however. For example, around the home, labels for homemade jams or herbs can be a good way to display your work practically; but

do remember to cover the work with sticky-back plastic to protect it. Or why not take a little more time over the writing of birthday and seasonal cards? Bookmarks, again laminated or sealed with sticky-back plastic, are a good way to enjoy your work on a daily basis. Re-writing your favourite poems, prose passages or even recipes are other ways of utilising and developing your skills.

One of the best ways to enjoy the craft and to perfect it would be to follow the example set by Edith Holden and begin a diary. Whether you choose to keep a nature diary like hers, or one recording memorable moments in your life or the lives of your family, it can give purpose and direction for your work and perhaps more importantly can be shared and enjoyed by future generations.

Tools of the Trade

One of the delights of calligraphy is how simple it is to get started.
A selection of good-quality calligraphy pens, ink, paper and a flat
surface to work on are all that are required.

The implements included in this set provide an excellent starting point and introduction to calligraphy but to get the most out of this art form you may wish to collate a more complete set of tools. The following items will certainly be of use as you find your feet:

- Dip penholders, nibs and reservoirs (these are tiny metal pieces which clip behind the nib of a dip pen to hold ink, see far right)

- Pencils – choose between HB to 2B

- Calligraphy felt-tip pens

- Brushes – fine sable for filling in colour between lines, cheap ones for loading paint onto pen nibs, and chisel-edged ones for drawing letter shapes

- Calligraphy inks – if you intend to decorate your work, ensure your ink is waterproof

- A pad of layout or tracing paper

- Watercolour and gouache paints

- Good cartridge paper for your finished calligraphy

- Ruler

- Eraser

- Distilled water and shell gold for gilding

- A jar of clean water for cleaning dip pens and brushes

- You will also need some rags for wiping your pen nibs. Use kitchen paper for mopping up spills, but not for wiping nibs, as shreds of paper can clog your nibs and brushes

- You may also like to buy a calligraphy fountain pen (these sometimes come in sets with a range of nibs and cartridges) for either right- or left-handers

Pens and Nibs

The pen is at the heart of all calligraphy. All calligraphic pens have nibs that can produce the characteristic thick and thin lines of the letter forms. Pens are available for both left- and right-handers. Right-handed pens have a straight-edged nib, while left-handed pens are angled to take into account how they will be held. It is best to try out a pen before buying if you can. You should look for a pen that produces a good strong contrast between thick and thin lines.

A good option for beginners is to use a felt-tip pen with a calligraphic nib. Felt-tips are easier to handle and make less mess, as well as delivering a more controlled supply of ink. Of course, they also do away with constant refilling; once they run out you simply dispose of the pen.

Fountain pens with calligraphic nibs appeal to the more traditionally minded. While the nibs are generally of higher quality than felt-tip pens, they do require careful maintenance. Fountain pens are available with either cartridges or reservoirs. Cartridge

Calligraphy nibs come in a multitude of different shapes and sizes.
Experiment and find the one that best suits your style.

11

pens are generally cheaper and offer a range of ink colours to choose from. Both types require cleaning after use to prevent dried ink from clogging the nib.

Experienced or ambitious calligraphers will choose a dip-nibbed pen. These pens commonly consist of a wooden shaft and a selection of interchangeable nibs. These nibs have to be constantly dipped into bottled ink. Dipping pens can also be used with thicker inks such as Chinese and Japanese ink sticks, that produce rich blacks and dense colours. These inks are not suitable for use with cartridge pens.

Chinese calligraphers favour brushes as they suit the letter forms of the Chinese alphabet. Brushes are very hard to master though and in the rest of this book we will be focusing on pen-based techniques.

Ink

If you are using felt-tip pens you won't need any ink as they come pre-filled, but if you have any other sort of pen, you will need to consider what ink to use.

Always make sure that the ink you choose is suitable for the type of pen you will be writing with. Dipping pens offer the widest choice of ink types – from standard inks, through to gouache paint and ink sticks.

Gouache is blended with water to the desired consistency and can be mixed together to create a wide range of colours.

Ink sticks are also mixed with water which is traditionally done on an inkstone available from most craft shops.

Paper

Paper is the third member of the calligraphic trinity. At the most basic level, any paper will do, but it is best to use a paper that does not bleed (that is, does not allow the ink to seep through to the other side of the paper).

For beginners, or when practising, inkjet or photocopier paper is perfectly suitable, but you will want to use a better quality paper to show off your final creations to their best and full effect.

The finest calligraphy should be displayed on the highest-quality paper. Ancient calligraphers often wrote on parchment or vellum (made from animal hides).

Watercolour is a particularly good choice, especially one with an even surface known as hot-pressed (HP). Textured surfaces may be interesting for large textural letters but can prove totally unsuited to fine writing.

It is best to use paper which is 190 gsm weight/thickness, alternatively you can opt for paper which doesn't wrinkle, such as 300 gsm.

Some handmade papers are perfect for calligraphy, their unique textures and subtle colour changes providing additional interest to your writing. The same is true of coloured paper, which can provide continuous smooth colour without requiring you to make a wash background. These may be hard to find today but most craft shops will stock ranges of fine or handmade papers that will be just right for that special project.

For a different feel you can also consider using fabrics or other materials, but these are likely to require specialist nibs.

Letter Basics

To produce the most beautiful calligraphy possible, you have to prepare yourself and your work area. Make sure all your materials are to hand, and remove any distractions such as the telephone. Take a deep breath and enjoy!

Getting Ready to Write

To produce the neatest writing it is necessary to be sitting comfortably. A sloping board will help you to sit up straight as you work.

The best angle between your pen nib and the line on which you are writing is 45 degrees. This means that the ink will be drawn from your pen by the flexing of the nib and not by gravity, resulting in more controlled letter forms.

You will also need a guard sheet taped to the bottom of the board. This allows the paper you are writing on to slide underneath, so that your hand remains in the same place all the time. Ideally this should be at about shoulder height.

You should make sure that you have a good source of even and bright light so you can see what you are writing clearly and to avoid eye strain.

Ancient calligraphers worked many long and hard hours at their manuscripts. You, however, should try to take regular breaks to avoid headaches, backache, wrist strain and other injuries.

Ergonomics

It is very important that you sit well when you are practising calligraphy. There is a story of a traditional calligrapher, Tang, who sat crooked and became a hunchback! Ensure that your back is straight, that you are not leaning on your arms and that your head is not too far forward.

As you gain confidence, you may find that you can control the pen best if you allow the pen body to rest against your knuckle, instead of in the 'V' between the thumb and forefinger. Your grip should be firm and still, allowing the nib to glide over the paper without pressing down on the pen.

Writing with a Calligraphy Pen

When you write with a normal pen you can move it in any direction. A calligraphy pen will only write in certain directions – it will not move upwards or to the left if you are writing with a right-handed pen, or to the right if you are using a left-handed pen.

To form the letters correctly you need to use separate strokes. Following the numbered sequence of arrows on the alphabets in this book will show you which strokes you need to form each individual letter.

Your First Efforts

There's one more hurdle to jump before producing your first words and letters. In order to get a feel for how your pen actually writes, the basic letter forms (shown on page 16) will allow you to experience the sensation of making calligraphic marks on paper for the first time.

Use a few sheets for practise. Don't worry about the occasional blob or scratch – just adjust the angle of your nib or pen and keep going.

Letter Forms

These practice letter forms (pictured below) show many of the basic shapes that you will need to master the style of your choice. Follow the directions as indicated by the arrows to familiarise yourself with these forms, and practise them until you can do them with ease. You can see samples of complete alphabets in various styles later on (pages 19–25).

Height of Letters

The height of your letters will depend on how wide your nib is. The wider the nib, the larger the letters. To work out how tall to make your letters, create a nib ladder by turning your paper sideways. Draw short alternate strokes on the edge of the paper, as shown here.

- - - - - ascender
- - - - - cap. height
——— x-height

——— baseline

- - - - - descender

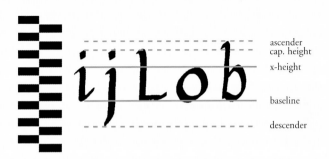

ascender
cap. height

x-height

baseline

descender

The height of the capital letters and letters with ascenders (where part of the letter goes up, for example b, d, t) should be slightly less than twice the size of the body of the letter. The descenders (where part of the letter goes down, for example j, g, p, y) should go down the same amount. A good average is to make the body of the letters four nib widths high from the baseline (to the x-height line), and the ascenders and descenders three nib widths.

Of course you can vary this, for example making the body five nib widths and the ascenders and descenders four nib widths. The height of these lower-case letters is called the x-height, because it is based on the height of the lower-case letter x.

The chart above shows the relative heights of letters and their component parts. Capital letters are normally slightly lower than the ascender heights. The bowls of the letter o and other similar letters should rest slightly under the baseline to avoid a floating look.

The most beautiful calligraphy has perfectly uniform letters. To achieve this in your own work you will need to practise, using either graph paper or by drawing pencil lines on paper to ensure that your letters are all of the same proportions.

There are many different alphabets that can be used in calligraphy, or you can even make up your own, but it's best if you're a beginner to start with an easy alphabet.

First Practice

Foundation hand, shown to the right, is a good first style to practise since it is clear and open.

With the height of letters taken into account in Letter Basics (pages 14–16), your first attempts should also show consideration to the width of your letters. As you learn and practise foundation hand, try thinking of your letter as fitting into a series of circles, squares and rectangles. Eventually this will become second nature to you.

Follow the sequence and direction of the arrows in each individual letter while you learn this and the subsequent alphabets.

Narrow Letters

Divide the circle in half to get the width of the narrow letters.

Round Letters

Round letters are based on a circle.

Rectangular Letters

Rectangular letters fit into the rectangle shown in red on top of the circle.

Wide Letters

Wide letters go outside the full circle. M has splayed verticals, meaning that the letter is wider at the bottom than it is at the top. W is the widest letter of all as it looks like two v shapes.

A B C D E
F G H I J K
L M N O P
Q R S T U
V W X Y Z
a b c d e
f g h i j k
l m n o p
q r s t u
v w x y z

Italic

The italic alphabet is easy to read and fairly easy to learn. The letters are quite narrow, and have oval curves. The slope of the letters can vary, so find a slope that suits you but make sure it is consistent in all of the letters.

Roman Capitals

These classical capital letters (also called majuscule) are based on those found on Trajan's Column in Rome, built in AD 114 to celebrate the emperor's victory over the Dacians. They work well with many forms of lower case (or minuscule) letters.

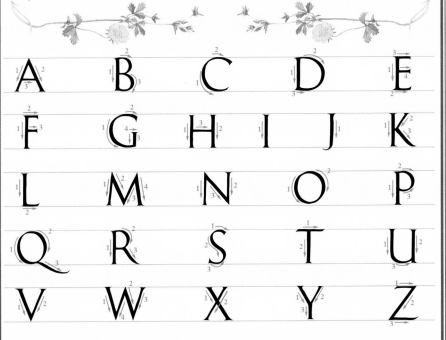

Uncials

To write this alphabet you need to change the angle of your pen so that the nib is angled more towards the horizontal (about 27 degrees). With the more rounded alphabets it is best to leave plenty of space between them or they can look crammed on the page.

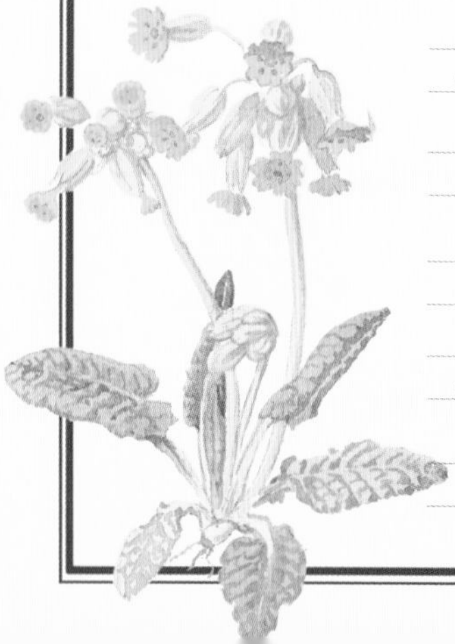

A B C D E
F G h i j k
L m n o p
q R s t u
v w x y z

a b c d e
f z h i j k
l m n o p
q R s t u
v w x y z

Rustica

Rustica is a style of writing which was used in ancient times for public notices since it could be easily drawn in a free manner on walls. Flowing more freely, and with greater verve, its letters stand more closely together than Roman capitals, and rustica letters are essentially taller than they are wide.

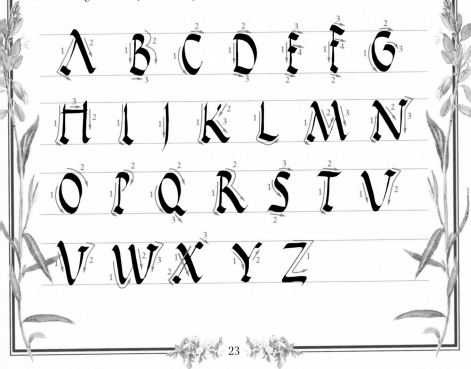

Gothic

This alphabet is less legible in blocks of text than either the Roman or italic alphabets, and is medieval in appearance. Work at a larger scale to begin with, as this will make it easier to learn the angles of the letters.

A B C D E
F G H I J K
L M N O P
Q R S T U
U W X Y Z

a b c d e
f g h i j k
l m n o p
q r s t u
v w x y z

Copperplate

Writing in copperplate requires a fine nib such as a gillot number 303 nib or a line mapping pen. Remember to use more pressure on the downward strokes and light pressure on hairline strokes. When practising try drawing lines at 55° as a guide to get the angle of the letters consistent.

Numerals

If you are going to be using numbers in calligraphy, some thought needs to be given to how they are going to fit in with the rest of the text. The numbers should blend with the letters to keep the piece balanced, and not disrupt the flow of the text.

Placing Numerals

There are different ways of placing numerals effectively into a text. This will depend to some extent on the type of writing that you are using.

If the lettering is all in capitals, putting numbers of the same height into the text will camouflage them within the piece.

Some numbers can also be written partly above or below the main body of the letters, just as ascending and descending letters are. The even numbers 4, 6 and 8 can be treated like ascenders, while the numbers 3, 5, 7 and 9 can be written like descenders.

Keep the numbers the same size as the letters, so that the natural flow of the text is maintained.

Using Numbers

Using numbers within your design can add interest to the layout if done well.

The letter forms of most numerals can easily be embellished with flourishes without losing legibility. Another trick with a collection of numbers, such as dates, is to vary the size of each number and its vertical placement to create pleasing interactions.

Look around for examples of interesting and original use of numerals and try to incorporate them into your work.

Almost all calligraphic hands did not have numerals originally associated with them for the simple reason that an entirely different Roman numbering system was used. The Roman numbering system uses letters instead of numerals, these can look

Numerals as Descenders

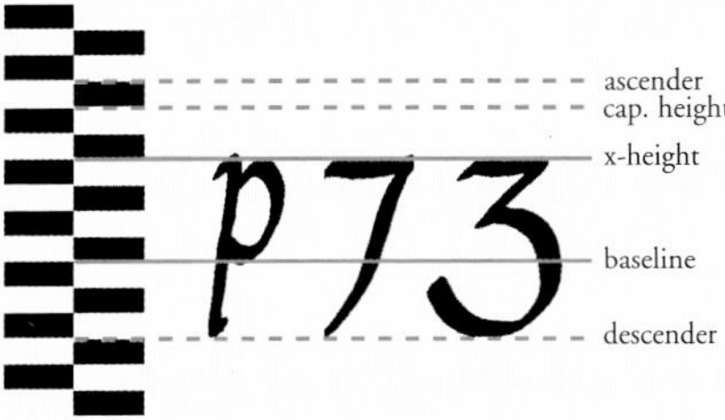

ascender
cap. height
x-height

baseline

descender

Numerals as Ascenders

ascender
cap. height
x-height

baseline

descender

Numerals at the Capital Height

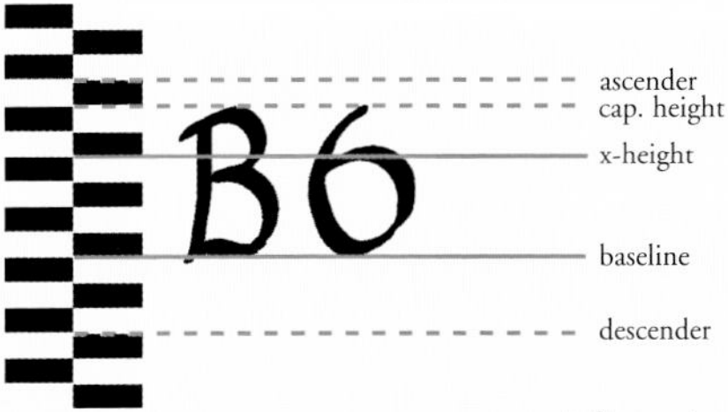

ascender
cap. height
x-height

baseline

descender

elegant and in keeping with your text so consider researching them from the internet or from the library.

The numerals below have been developed in latter years to meet the needs of modern calligraphers and can be used with a variety of different hands.

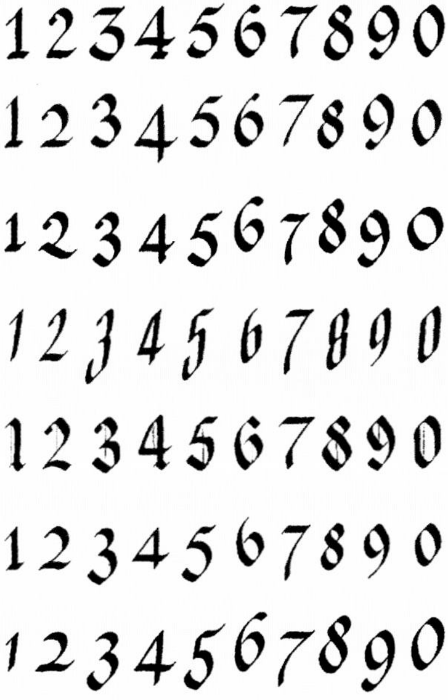

1234567890
1234567890
1234567890
1234567890
1234567890
1234567890
1234567890

Flourishes

Once you've become experienced at writing one or several alphabets, you can try your hand at flourishes. These are elaborate extensions of letters. They may be added to one or more characters in a piece of writing, and are often used for formal texts, but can feature anywhere to add flair to the piece.

When creating flourishes bear the following points in mind:

• Your basic letter shapes must be well-formed, and the flourish should be an extension of the letter and not an addition to it.

• Flourishes should reflect the nature of the text you are writing, and should appear to be part of the natural flow of the piece.

• Make sure that the letter is legible and that the flourish doesn't obscure any other letters.

• When planning the layout of your work, take into account any flourishes that you are going to make, considering where they are going to be, and how much space they will take up.

Practising Flourishes

You will need plenty of practice to produce flourishes with ease.

Start practising by crossing thick and thin lines, running them both diagonally and parallel to each other.

Try to keep your hand relaxed so that the lines flow naturally. Thin strokes are normally formed with an upward stroke, while thicker strokes can be made by applying more pressure on downward strokes. Begin with simple shapes before going on to more elaborate designs.

A selection of shapes to practise is shown on the next page. Once you are confident with the feel of flourishes you can add them to the letter forms of your choice.

These flourishes are similar to those often found on bank notes

Spirals make interesting flourishes

You can easily combine flourishes to create more complex ones

Remember to lift your pen when you change direction

Interlocking or overlapping flourishes make interesting shapes

Monograms

As a personal, or finishing touch, monograms can be the perfect vehicle for practising flourishes.

Try designing a monogram with one, or more, of your initials.

This may, or may not, include a flourish. Some combinations are fraught with problems before you begin – IV can look like an arrow or a badly drawn N, while initials which spell out a word need twisting to conceal the word.

Work in rough and with different pen thicknesses until you find a solution.

Layout Techniques

Now that you have the letters and spacing right, it is time to lay your words out on a page. The layout of the words on a page is just as important as the words themselves.

Before you begin creating an actual project, you need to think about how you are going to lay out your page. Decide on which script you are going to use, whether some of the letters or words will be larger than the others, and whether you will use colour.

The easiest way to start is with a simple layout. Choose the size of your nib depending on how much text you need to write. If there is a lot of text to fit in, choose a smaller nib size and vice versa.

If you want the lines to be more or less the same length, you can contract or expand letters or words to make them fit in, or perhaps write key words in capitals (see page 41).

Make sure that you leave plenty of space in the margins so that the text does not look too cramped. The easiest way of laying out the wording is with a straight margin on the left.

Other layouts can look more interesting, such as each line centred or balanced around a central line, giving your work a 'spine'.

Try to keep some balance to the layout; don't allow it to become too top- or bottom-heavy. Varying the size of the letters can add interest, but avoid too many changes as this does not allow for smooth reading.

A practical tip is to write out the project in your chosen hand and actual size, cut out each line separately and use these lines to align the text and experiment with the layout; see the featured projects for more information.

Remember that simple is often the best. Overloading the page with too much text, colour, or differing sizes letters and script can make the page look messy, so that is it difficult for the reader to focus on the text.

Regular borders, well spaced

Borders too narrow

Aligned left pages are easy to write

Centred pages make interesting shapes

Balanced pages need a visual 'spine' to work

Different letter sizes add interest

Headings

Headings can be emphasised in different ways. Whether you choose to make the lettering bold, colourful, elaborately decorated or to combine several of these elements, it should stand out from the rest of the text. Headings should be placed slightly apart from the main wording but they don't always have to be at the top of the text. For example, you could run a heading down one side, or place it at the bottom of the page, or even run it obliquely across the middle of the piece.

Before writing out your piece, it is best to design the page first, deciding what the heading should be, how big to write it, and where to place it. Work it out in rough first, so that you can balance all the elements. Rule off the area that will contain the text to get a feel for the finished effect.

If you are including subheadings in your text, think about how they will relate both to the heading and to the rest of the text.

Try to link your ideas so that the heading and subheadings have something in common. For example, use the same decoration or style of writing for the subheading as you used for the heading, but make it smaller and simplify the decoration.

Straightforward heading and subheading

Experiment with your use of heading and subheading

Try using landscape layouts

31

Borders

Placing a border around your calligraphy text can add greatly to the overall appearance of the piece. Before placing a border around your work you need to decide whether this will complement, and not detract from, the overall effect. If you feel that it will be of benefit, then some additional planning of the layout and design is needed.

Illuminated manuscripts often had decorative borders as well as beautiful versals (oversized initials).

Borders have been used to beautify and add importance to many passages of text, throughout the centuries.

Space is important on a page, so make sure you know the area needed for the main body of text. Write it out carefully on another sheet, cut out each line and transfer their measurements to the paper you will use for the finished work.

Unless incorporating small pictures that reflect the subject matter of your text, the four basic elements to a border are: dots, horizontal, vertical and diagonal lines. Experiment with different combinations of these four elements and mix techniques and materials to create striking borders.

First decide what sort of border you are going to use – is it going to surround the text completely? Will it be regular or irregular? How will the corners work? If your border is going to surround the text, either partially or completely, the best place to start is at the corner.

There are three basic ways of organising the corners of your borders: oblique, square and joggled mitre. The type to use will depend on your design and the style of border you are producing.

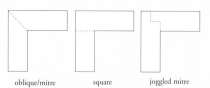

oblique/mitre   square   joggled mitre

Design your border in rough first, pencilling in the areas or spaces where the text will be, then work out your border size and design around this. Try experimenting with different tools and colours to see the different effects you can create. Use either a single tool (for example, a brush or pen) or colour, or a combination of tools and/or colours, and let your creativity flow.

What type of border?

The type of border you use should relate in some way to the piece of writing, whether it reflects elements of the subject matter or the style of writing used. There are many different elements of border design including spots, horizontal, vertical, oblique and lettered. These can be used singly or in combination to produce a pattern. If you choose a lettered border make sure you pick letters that work well together visually.

Pattern borders can be enlivened with careful use of spot colours

Use shapes to evoke the theme of your piece. For example, star shapes around a poem about the night sky.

A repeated tracing of your favourite plant image can look professional and elegant.

A rural scene can add depth fun to your project and bring with it a sense of charming simplicity.

Illumination and Gilding

The early western scribes were also artists, and added colour and gilding to their work, often using the first letter of a page or paragraph to show off their skills. Look for some examples of early decorated work to see how it was done, and to develop ideas of your own.

There are many different ways of illustrating or illuminating letters. You can either fill in the spaces within the letters, decorate them, or make the decoration actually form the letter.

To begin with you need to think about the text you are using, and relate this to the illuminated letter. Think also about the letter shape. If it is elongated, such as an f, this could be extended downwards to form a border for the paragraph.

Some letters, such as o, e or n, can be enclosed in a box or square, and the inner space decorated. The letter can either be left plain or worked into the overall design.

Planning your Decorations

At first, your decoration should be simple. It is best to design your letter in rough first, trying to keep it as near to the finished size as possible. Try to allow the decoration to flow freely, and stick to one or two patterns to begin with.

It is usually best to do this in pencil first, so that you can correct any mistakes. Once this is done the work can be decorated using pencil, ink, paint or gilding.

You could do a tracing of a letter you've come across and reproduce it, changing the design to suit the theme of your piece. Consider the overall effect of the illustration and remember, it is better to under-decorate than over-decorate. Try copying the letter 'B' for practice.

Materials

- Tracing paper
- Set square
- HP watercolour paper

- Low-tack masking tape
- H pencil and rubber
- Watercolour brushes size 0 and 1 and another 0 for the shell gold
- Distilled water
- Shell gold (gold powder suspended in a solution, 'Jaune' is traditional gold)
- Agate burnisher
- Watercolour paints: burnt sienna, Vandyke brown, cadmium lemon, alizarin crimson, cobalt blue

Method

1. First of all you will need to accurately trace an enlarged photocopy of the letter B. With the tracing paper over your photocopy, use the set square to draw a right angle onto your tracing paper and on your watercolour paper – first working out where you want the position of your letter to go. Place the tracing paper over your chosen design and tape it down with low-tack masking tape. Draw over it with a your pencil – remember to carefully trace the rounded sections. Also check that you can see where the leaves and stems overlap the gold; these areas

must be left blank whilst gilding. Turn the tracing paper over and draw the outline on the reverse as well. Now place your finished

tracing on top of your project paper, lining it up with the right angles and making sure it is straight with your page. Secure with tape. Scribble over the back of the tracing paper with a pencil and ensure that all the design has been completely transferred over.

2. Use the size 0 brush to add a small amount of distilled water to the edge of the shell gold. Holding the gold at an angle, mix until it is still runny but does not look transparent. Test on a spare piece of paper. Leave a few brush marks of gold to dry,

then gently burnish with the agate burnisher; if the gold becomes shiny you have the right mix. (Too little gold in the mix and it will look a pale brown on the paper, whereas too much gold will look gritty and neither will burnish.) When you have the right mix, slowly brush the gold onto the B, working from the edges inwards. As it is a suspension, you will need to re-mix the gold, each time adding more water or gold before applying. Leave to dry.

3. Gently rub the gold using small strokes of the agate burnisher until it shines.

4. You can paint the flowers with your own selection of colours or use the following instructions. It is important to consider depth and shade and to plan the colours before you start. You must rub out the pencil marks before you begin painting the flowers and check that the widths and direction of all stems and leaves line up where they cross over or behind something else.

5. Dog Roses: paint the flower centres a light cadmium yellow and paint the petals with a size 1 brush with a mix of pale scarlet and a touch of cadmium yellow. Add shading to the leaves and stems using a mix

of cadmium yellow and cobalt blue. Add more scarlet lake to the petals, leaving some areas, with just one layer of paint, to create depth. Paint the stamens using mixes of either cadmium yellow or yellow ochre and burnt sienna.

6. Violets and Heartsease: use a mix of cobalt blue and alizarin crimson to apply the first layer of colour to the violets. Use this same mix to paint the upper petals of the heartsease flowers, fading the colour off from the centre of the petals. Mix a lighter mauve for the middle flowers and add a touch of cadmium yellow where the petal

touches near the centre. Add cadmium yellow to the lower petal of the heartsease flowers, leaving space for highlights towards the left side.

7. Primroses: use pale cadmium lemon paint for the petals, adding further layers for depth and shape. Shade, particularly where petals overlap, is added using a pale sap green mixed with cadmium lemon. Give the leaves a wash of the cadmium yellow and add shade with a blue/green mix of cadmium lemon and cobalt blue.

8. Check to see what flowers on your illuminated letter need depth and colour added. Now focus on the leaves and stems. Using a size 0 brush, begin creating definition by adding shade to the right side of the stems and under leaves with a little French ultramarine mixed with sap green. Add colour to the leaves and the rest of the stems using a size 0 brush and a pale mix of sap green to give a tinge of colour. Some leaves and petals may be left pale and undetailed behind the B, which will add a sense of distance.

9. With a size 0 brush, outline the gilded B with Vandyke brown; make it slightly thicker on the right-hand sides of the uprights, curves and lines.

10. Add shadows with burnt sienna where a stem or shadow crosses the gold sections of the gilded B. With a size 0 brush mix a little white with a pale greeny yellow and add the centres of the primroses and heartsease flowers. Finally, check the painting to make sure any little details have not been left out.

Bookmark

Making your own bookmark is easy if you follow these simple steps, and when you finish, you'll have the perfect showcase for your new-found skills.

Materials

- Card and layout or scrap paper
- Ruler
- Pencil
- Eraser
- Scissors
- Number 3 nib and a Number 4 nib
- Reservoir and pen holder
- Tracing paper
- Low-tack masking tape
- Mapping pen and nib
- Brown sepia ink
- Hole punch (optional)
- Ribbon (optional)
- Sticky-back plastic (optional)

Method

1. Cut your card to a suitable size for your bookmark. Measure and gently mark a pencil line in the middle.

2. With any calligraphy it is important to plan the layout of your text (see page 30–31). For the best positioning and composition first write the quote out on layout paper. In the example on page 39 the quote is written using a number 3 nib, with five nib widths for the italic hand. The author's name is written in Roman capitals using a number 4 nib, seven widths high. Your choice of nib sizes depends on the size of your bookmark.

3. Cut out each line separately from your rough layout, as close as possible to the writing. Fold the lines in half to find the centre points in the text. Marry these up with the line on your bookmark and gently mark the ends of the lines and their widths.

4. Now start writing the text in italic and Roman capitals on the bookmark. Allow the ink to dry completely.

5. The border in this example is easy to replicate, or you can design your own. Begin by covering your calligraphy with tracing paper, to avoid smudging, and secure with tape. Follow the tracing instructions as laid out on page 35, but make sure you measure and incorporate the floral element in the border. Lift one edge of your tracing to check all the design is transferred. Using the pencil go over the design firmly but not so hard that you indent the paper.

6. Using the mapping pen, ink in the design by creating the stems and outlining the leaves. Practising on a spare piece of paper first is helpful to feel the flow of the design.

7. Complete the border section by filling in the leaves with sepia ink. Erase any

remaining pencil markings from the bookmark and border.

8. For finishing touches you could punch a hole through the top and thread with a ribbon. Protect your bookmark with sticky-back plastic if you wish.

Literature is the immortality of speech

AUGUST WILHELM VON SCHLEGEL (1767 ~ 1845)

Decorated Poem

A poem decorated with an illuminated letter and elegant calligraphy would make a wonderful gift – especially a romantic one. You could even present your favourite poem in this way and hang it on your wall.

Materials

- Layout paper
- Hard pencil (H), eraser and scissors
- Ruler and set square
- Low-tack masking tape
- HP watercolour paper – no less than 300 gsm weight – and tracing paper
- Calligraphy pen
- Distilled water
- Shell gold, 'Jaune'
- Sepia or black ink
- Agate burnisher
- Watercolour brushes: size 0 and 2 and a second size 0 brush for the shell gold
- Watercolour paints: cadmium red, alizarin crimson, sap green, cobalt blue, manganese blue, burnt sienna and Vandyke brown.

Method

1. Roughly sketch your illuminated letter and poem onto your layout paper. Experiment with the positioning of the illuminated letter in relation to the text – think about having it above or in the first line. Consider the length of the lines and how to justify and align the text as well.

2. Write out the poem in uncials onto your layout paper. Cut out each line and experiment with their position: try them close together as well as wide apart. In this example all but the opening lines are the

same length; to balance the lines, the words 'love' and 'roses' can be written in capitals to lengthen the line and place romantic emphasis on these words. Try it in pencil first. If you want to alter the length of a line write it last so you can work to a size.

3. Cut out a rough, same-size design of the illuminated letter to use as a guide while you write. Now write the poem on your watercolour paper. Use pencil guidelines and the mid-points in the lines to get the position right (see page 38). Allow the ink to dry. Cover the poem with tracing paper while you work on the illuminated letter.

4. The design of your illuminated letter will depend upon the subject of your poem and the letter you've chosen to decorate. In each case you will need to work from a detailed drawing or image (actual size) from which you can trace the design. See page 35 for tracing instructions. Take note of the areas where

elements intertwine: for example where the roses intersect the stem, and the leaves intersect the letter. Make sure these are obvious on the tracing.

5. Go over the tracing with a fine pointed pencil checking that all the image has been transferred. Check that you can see clearly where the gaps are in the gilding for the painted roses, leaves and stems. These areas must be left blank when gilding.

6. Begin the gilding (see pages 35–36).

7. After burnishing the gilding, paint the floral detail using another size 0 brush. First paint the rose outlines with cadmium red then shade towards the base of the petals with alizarin crimson. Mix sap green with some cobalt blue and paint the stems and leaves, including those that go in the spaces across or behind the gilding. Add shading to the stems and leaves with more cobalt blue added to the green.

8. Tint the background by mixing a dilute manganese blue wash. Test on a piece of layout paper. Brush clean water inside and around the R and flowers using your size 2 brush – get as close as you can and use only enough to dampen the paper. Cover the damp area with the coloured wash. As it dries sweep another layer lightly around the edges of the R and the roses. Then sweep another line around the edge of the outer shape.

9. When the wash has dried add detail to the leaves by painting in veins, edges and little strokes to give the leaves a serrated outline. Deepen the shadows where leaves cross under each other or disappear behind the R. Add small thorns to the rose stems with cadmium red and sap green.

10. Paint the shadows left by the overlapping roses, stems and leaves onto the gold – using a dry-brush technique (if the paint is too wet it will ruin the gilding) apply burnt sienna with a size 0 brush.

11. With Vandyke brown paint a smaller area, on top of the burnt sienna around the flowers. This creates a greater 3-D effect.

12. To outline the gilded letter and the background surrounding it, use a size 0 brush and a dilution of manganese blue. Rub out any pencil lines to finish.

ROSES

You LOVE the ROSES~so do I. I wish
The sky would rain down roses, as they rain
From off the shaken bush. Why will it not?
Then all the valley would be pink and white
And soft to tread on. They would fall as light
As feathers, smelling sweet; and it would be
Like sleeping and like waking, all at once!

GEORGE ELIOT (1819 ~ 1880)

Wedding Invitation

Add an extra-special personal touch to a wedding by designing the invitations yourself. You can experiment with all sorts of different styles, just keep your eyes open and look out for ideas.

Materials

- Layout paper and tracing paper
- Paper glue
- Ruler
- Scissors
- Nib holder and mapping pen
- Pencil
- Eraser
- Goatskin parchment or cartridge paper
- Sepia or black ink
- Adjustable set square for tracing
- Watercolour brushes; size 0, 1 and 2
- Watercolour paints: scarlet lake, cadmium lemon, cerulean blue, yellow ochre, Vandyke brown, Davy's grey, Payne's grey, cobalt blue, cadmium scarlet, French ultramarine.

Method

1. Plan out your design on layout paper first, ensuring you will have enough room on your final piece for the decorative elements. Once satisfied, write out the invitation in copperplate (see page 25) onto layout paper using your mapping pen. Cut out each of the lines. Fold and mark the mid-point on each of the sentences. On a separate piece of layout paper stick down each line, marrying up the mid-points to

Mr George Smith & Mrs Carol Smith
request the pleasure of your company
at the marriage of their daughter
Marie Hannah
to
Mr Stephen Johns
on Saturday 10th June 2006 at 2pm
at St Mary's Church, Middleton
and afterwards at the Bell Hotel

44

centre-align the invitation; left-aligning the 'rsvp' to the bottom left-hand corner and a thoughtful quote in the bottom right-hand corner.

2. Choose the paper you want to use for your final piece. Cartridge paper will look good but you may choose to use a cream-coloured paper.

3. Referring to the rough design, draw light guidelines onto your final paper. These should indicate the start, end and mid-points of the sentences. It is also advisable to draw horizontal lines to keep the text perfectly straight. When you're ready, write out your final piece in sepia or black ink. Allow it to dry then rub out the pencil marks.

4. Trace the cherubs by following the instructions on page 35. Begin painting the cherubs' bodies using a size 1 brush and a light mix of scarlet lake with a tiny amount of cadmium lemon – you are aiming for a flesh tint. Add more shading to the right sides of the cherubs as if light is coming from the left and also where the cherubs' arms and hands meet. Using a light wash of cadmium lemon paint in the hair. Give the wings a pale wash of cerulean blue.

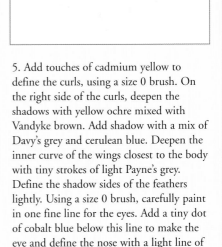

5. Add touches of cadmium yellow to define the curls, using a size 0 brush. On the right side of the curls, deepen the shadows with yellow ochre mixed with Vandyke brown. Add shadow with a mix of Davy's grey and cerulean blue. Deepen the inner curve of the wings closest to the body with tiny strokes of light Payne's grey. Define the shadow sides of the feathers lightly. Using a size 0 brush, carefully paint in one fine line for the eyes. Add a tiny dot of cobalt blue below this line to make the eye and define the nose with a light line of the scarlet lake. Use a little scarlet lake to paint in the mouth.

6. Using the standard tracing method, trace off the border and tape in place to fit

around the calligraphy. Match a central line on your tracing with a central line on the watercolour paper.

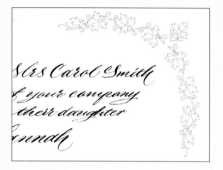

7. Remove as much pencil from the transferred image as is possible. Mix cadmium lemon and cobalt blue to make a mid-green colour. Using a size 0 brush, outline the leaves and stems. With a size 1 brush paint in the stems and leaves. Use a size 0 brush to paint the single curved lines at one end of the border. Using a size 0 brush and a bluer mix of the green, paint in the veins on the leaves. Along the edge of each leaf, stem and connecting decoration, add a line of darker green on

the right-hand side, to create depth and shadow. With a size 0 brush paint the berries using cadmium scarlet.

8. With a size 0 brush and French ultramarine, deepen the small shadows where the stems pass under a leaf, the curves at the bases of the leaves and where

the berries join the stems. Add dark green to the single lines at the one end of the decoration.

9. Ensure that it is completely dry before attempting to remove any more pencil lines. Instead of writing this out many times, consider going to a professional printers and getting them to print as many copies as you need; it shouldn't cost that much and it could save you a lot of time.

Mr George Smith & Mrs Carol Smith
request the pleasure of your company
at the marriage of their daughter

Marie Hannah

to

Mr Stephen Johns

on Saturday 10th June 2006, at 2pm
at St Mary's Church, Middleton
and afterwards at The Bell Hotel

R.S.V.P.
Mrs C Smith
9 Station Lane
Middleton
By 30.4.06

To Love is to place our happiness in the
happiness of another
Gottfried Wilhelm von Leibniz
1646 ~ 1716

47

Conclusion

In our modern world, as people turn more and more to computers and e-mail to communicate, many people are finding refuge in the varied and skilled world of calligraphy.

The enthusiast who has tried out everything in this book is a beginner no longer, but a seasoned craftsperson who is probably, by now, fighting off requests for hand-drawn lettering of all kinds. If you have the time to work on something for yourself, consider these ideas:

- Painted china, favourite recipes or commemorative plates for wedding anniversaries.

- Calligraphy can look great alongside stencils in your own home. Try mixing an image with carefully planned words or quotes along a dull piece of wall.

- A family tree with the bride and groom's ancestry, for their wedding present.

- A book of an elderly relative's favourite reminiscences.

All these projects will increase your skills but why not try out the intricacies of Celtic scrollwork, and use it to decorate your illuminated letters?

Try using different inks, and other alphabets – make up your own alphabets too. Experiment with different papers.

Keep practising and look out for examples of calligraphy wherever you go. Calligraphy can be applied to many surfaces, it is just a question of choosing one – the rest is up to your imagination!

Remember, Edith Holden did not become the revered artist she is today without things often going wrong; so if you smudge the paint and have to start again, know that the next time it will be even better.

THE COUNTRY DIARY®

Other titles available in the range are:

The Country Diary of an Edwardian Lady

Painting with Watercolours

Stencilling

Herbal Remedies

Calligraphy

Flower Pressing

Cross Stitch

Learn to Paint Wildlife

Learn to Draw Nature

www.kudosbooks.com